Understanding Strategy
in a week

**BOB NORTON AND
RAY IRVING**

Hodder & Stoughton

A MEMBER OF THE HODDER HEADLINE GROUP

Orders: please contact Bookpoint Ltd, 130 Milton Park, Abingdon, Oxon OX14
4SB. Telephone: (44) 01235 400414, Fax: (44) 01235 400454. Lines are open from
9.00 - 6.00, Monday to Saturday, with a 24 hour message answering service.
Email address: orders@bookpoint.co.uk

British Library Cataloguing in Publication Data
A catalogue record for this title is available from The British Library

ISBN 0 340 72494 3

First published 1999
Impression number   10 9 8 7 6 5 4
Year   2004 2003 2002 2001

Typeset by Multiplex Techniques Ltd, St Mary Cray, Kent.
Printed in Great Britain for Hodder & Stoughton Educational, a division of
Hodder Headline Plc, 338 Euston Road, London NW1 3BH by Cox & Wyman Ltd,
Reading, Berkshire.

in the Institute of Management

The Institute of Management (IM) is the leading organisation for professional management. Its purpose is to promote the art and science of management in every sector and at every level, through research, education, training and development, and representation of members' views on management issues.

This series is commissioned by IM Enterprises Limited, a subsidiary of the Institute of Management, providing commercial services.

Management House,
Cottingham Road,
Corby,
Northants NN17 1TT
Tel: 01536 204222;
Fax: 01536 201651
Website: http://www.inst-mgt.org.uk

Registered in England no 3834492
Registered office: 2 Savoy Court, Strand,
London WC2R 0EZ

C O N T E N T S

Strategy – what you do – and planning – how you do it, became amalgamated into strategic planning in the 1960s and 1970s. As businesses searched for more and more ways of achieving a lead over the competition, strategic planning became identified with models, mystery and mumbo jumbo as a preserve of the corporate planners, and very soon took on a life of its own.

In the topsy-turvy environment of the late 1980s and the 1990s, strategic planning failed to adapt and reinvent itself in the new business climate that was emerging, and failed to deliver its inherent promise: a future direction for the organisation.

Understanding Strategy in a Week separates strategy from planning, selects the best of the established methods, combines them with the new, and redefines what organisations have to tackle to create an effective strategy for the future.

Understanding Strategy in a Week traces the following developments:

Sunday	Introducing strategy
Monday	Strategic models
Tuesday	Strategists and strategies
Wednesday	Strategic analysis
Thursday	Strategic thinking
Friday	From strategy to action
Saturday	Formulating strategy

Introducing strategy

But there can be no fixed rules, for there are endless permutations, variations and surprises on the battlefield. As in the game of chess, one has to continuously profit from the varied experiences gained. Each confrontation with the enemy has in it lessons even for the most seasoned of warriors.

Reminiscences of an Ancient Strategist: the Mind of Sun Tzu, Foo Check Teck, Gower, 1997, p. 11

Traditional methods of developing strategy no longer 'fit' in the ever-changing environment in which organisations operate. There is a new approach to formulating strategy, and a new set of 'rules' has emerged which can mean the difference between success and failure.

Throughout this week, we will explore this new approach to strategy to understand how best to move forward in a business climate where the old rules no longer apply.

Today, we shall look at strategy by addressing a number of frequently asked questions:

- What is strategy?
- Why do we need strategy?
- What does strategy involve?
- What strategy isn't
- Where strategy fits

What is strategy?

There are many definitions of strategy, and the more there
are, the more they tend to confuse rather than clarify. Most
respectable dictionaries will tell us that the origins of the
term 'strategy' are to be found in ancient Greek:

> *Strategia*: generalship, command of an army
>
> *Stratos*: an army
>
> *Agein*: to lead

Strategy, therefore, has its origins in generalship and the art or
science of conducting a military campaign or manoeuvring an
army. The term 'strategy' entered business language only after
the Second World War when military leaders on both sides of
the Atlantic came together to see if some of the successful
elements of waging war could be applied to business.

These origins help to clarify a question which continues to cause confusion in the business domain: is strategy *what we do,* or is it *how we do it?*

A return to military origins can help, this time with the Encyclopaedia Britannica:

Theory and conduct of strategy have traditionally been distinguished from tactics in the following ways: strategy deals with the entire theatre of war and the use of battles to win war, whereas tactics are concerned primarily with the use of troops and equipment to win battles, and the handling of troops on the battlefield.

In war, strategy deals with the overall formulation of campaigns prior to engagements on the battlefield. Tactics concern the actual manoeuvres, the specific actions to win the battle. Tactics are often called *sub-strategies* or *operational strategies.*

In football, the goal is victory by outscoring the opposing team. The game plan to achieve this goal is the strategy. The dead-ball free kick may be a tactic within the overall strategy.

Let us therefore establish our definition from the start:

> Strategy is about what we want to do, what we want our organisation to be and where we want it to go.

Tactics and planning are concerned with *how* we do things once we have decided *what* to do. Strategy and planning are not the same things: the former precedes the latter. This week, we address strategy.

Why do we need strategy?

The simple answer is that we cannot know where we are going without it.

All organisations get bogged down in routine tasks and the natural comfort of sticking to the way that things have always been done. This is because these have worked in the past. The ritual of simply trying to get things done can, however, make us forget exactly what we are trying to achieve and where we are trying to go.

Strategic thinking and change

If you take some time to consider the major changes that have taken place in your market over the last five or ten years, would you have possibly been able to foresee them? Maybe yes, maybe no. Maybe some.

More importantly, though, ask yourself if, ten years ago, you gave yourself the time to consider what the major changes would be over the next ten years. If you had, would your organisation now be in a better position?

Strategy provides an organisation with a framework for:

- understanding its position in the marketplace
- moving forward with a sense of direction, purpose and urgency
- focusing on the key issues of customers and markets, and on the skills needed to deliver to those customers and markets

A strategy should:

- make an organisation stand out from the competition
- make people sit up and take note
- capture the imagination and commitment of the workforce
- have a significant impact on the market

The only organisations that do not need a strategy are those which have no competitors, are in total control of their destiny, remain unaffected by changes in the marketplace, and occupy an environment that never changes.

Strategy, therefore, is essential for every organisation, large or small, public or private, service or manufacturing. On Tuesday, we shall look at some strategies that address – or are driven by – these factors.

What does strategy involve?

As we have said, strategy is about shaping the future. This involves addressing a number of questions:

1 Where are we now and how did we get here? What did we do well, or badly, to arrive at our current position?
2 What business are we in? Will this remain the same, or will we need to change our business? If so, to what? What factors internal and external to the organisation will, or can, have a telling impact on what we do in the future? These questions are principally about the first phase of formulating a strategy – strategic analysis – which we look at on Wednesday.
3 Where do we want to be in the future? We attempt to address this on Thursday when we look at what is involved in strategic thinking.

Only when we have addressed these questions, can we start tackling the question that has preoccupied planners for decades: how are we going to get there? Implementing a strategy is primarily about managing change, which we look at on Friday.

The continuing strategic process

One criticism levelled at strategic planning is that the future is too uncertain for us to predict. Locking an organisation into a *plan* causes problems when things change. The problem now, as we know, is that the pace of change no longer allows us to plan 15, 10 or even 5 years ahead. The three questions raised above are no longer to be asked every two, three or five years, but continually. The strategic process we propose during the week attempts to build in flexibility and continuity to anticipate and embrace change, instead of fear it and respond reactively.

Strategy and time

In an age when old-fashioned strategic planning –
involving a few of the senior elite closeting themselves
away for the annual weekend – has been discredited,
strategy is very much about making time for people to
make a contribution. If you think that developing a strategy
in this way is costly, then weigh up the costs of being
caught unprepared for changes in the marketplace. We take
a closer look at how strategic planning was dislodged from
its pedestal on Monday, and look at finding the time for
people to participate in the strategic process on Thursday.

What strategy isn't

One of the most well-known strategic bibles of the 1980s
was *In Search Of Excellence* by Peters and Waterman. It had
a significant impact on how people thought about the way
organisations did things (even though many of the

companies researched for the model of excellence fell from grace during the 1980s).

The excellence model encouraged organisations to examine concepts of quality and customer service and laid the foundation for many schemes – Total Quality Management (TQM), benchmarking, partnering, outsourcing, delayering and business process re-engineering (BPR) among them – which dominated corporate thinking in the 1980s and into the 1990s.

These schemes have produced operational improvements for the many organisations that adopted them. They all work, however, in the same direction, towards improving how things are done, cutting costs, and greater efficiencies in performing activities. As more organisations adopted them, so standards improved, raising quality for the customer..

WE'RE DOWN TO ZERO DEFECTS, BUT NO-ONE'S BUYING THEM!

If every organisation benchmarked for best practice, competitive advantage would ultimately be nullified because every organisation would be 'excellent' – performing similar activities very efficiently. But operational efficiency does not add up to business strategy.

- TQM can lead to improvements in operational efficiency but not a new strategic direction for the organisation
- BPR provides a process for reorganising how a company operates, but it won't – without some other source of inspiration and effort – galvanise management along a strategic path for the future.
- Benchmarking shows you how to catch up with the best today, but won't – on its own – create pioneers or new strategies.

We take a closer look at strategic models on Monday.

Where strategy fits

So where does strategy fit, and how does it relate to planning and managing change? Quite simply, strategy is at the top, and nothing can really start in earnest until the strategy is in place.

In business, strategy involves forming a path for the organisation to follow that will lead to products or services that customers will want. This will usually mean some kind of new departure for the business, requiring the leader to implement various tactics or sub-strategies. These tactics are usually set out in the component parts of the business plan.

So, strategy – and what you need to do to prepare the organisation before planning takes a hold – fits something like this.

Figure 1.

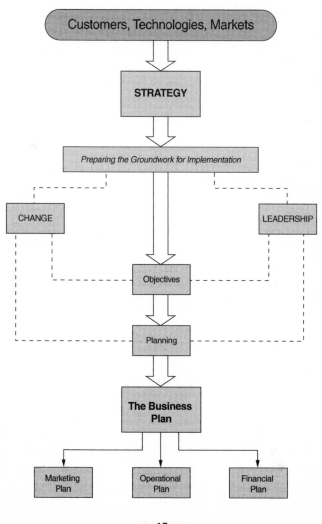

The business plan, a consequence of strategy, is the subject of a companion book in this series.

This week, we are concerned with formulating strategy and preparing the groundwork for its implementation. Principally, implementation is about how well leaders harness the resources at their disposal to start turning the strategy into reality. We look at preparing the strategy for action on Friday.

On Saturday we present a summary review of the strategy-formulation process, highlighting the key points and principles illustrated during the week.

Summary

A strategy needs to be:

- consistent so that staff and customers identify with what you are trying to deliver to them, but flexible so that the strategy can exploit change and adapt to it
- responsive to market and environmental conditions and not merely led by them
- creative so that it inspires commitment, but not so 'visionary' that it seems remote
- challenging so that it requires effort to attain, but realistic and achievable
- focused so that it is clear, defined and understandable to staff and customers, but not cast in stone

As all organisations are different, no two strategies are the same. We all have different strengths and weaknesses, we all spot different opportunities in different ways, and we all operate in different ways from one another. Strategies then will differ from one organisation to another, but the process of formulating strategy is similar for all.

Today we have attempted to distinguish the meaning of strategy from the process of planning and implementation. The 1970s and 1980s produced many models to facilitate the strategic process. We look at these models tomorrow and judge how applicable they are to the present day.

Strategic models

> *... each firm was working by trial and error, and all too often repeating the errors of others rather than learning from them.*
>
> *Management and Machiavelli*, Antony Jay,
> Hodder & Stoughton, 1967, p. 16

Today we look at various models designed to provide organisations with methods and systems for gaining advantage over the competition. We begin by asking where the models came from, and we conclude today by examining their legacy. We look at:

- where strategic models came from
- the models
- how the models worked
- what changed?
- why the models are no longer enough
- what the models don't tell you

Where strategic models came from

The concept of strategy was launched into a business world that was rebuilding and recovering after the Second World War. A long period of deprivation meant that consumer goods were hard to come by and choice was not on the shopping list.

It was a period when new technology meant heavy machinery to reduce the grind of factory-floor processes, and when organisations grew in size, placing layers of bureaucracy between those who set the tasks to be done and those who did them. Inflation had no major significance for business planning or budgeting, and markets were relatively stable. What was produced was sold, and consumers 'who had never had it so good' were largely content with what was available, indeed to have it at all.

If there was one single catalyst for change which destroyed the old order – but failed to replace it with a new – it was probably the Oil Crisis of 1974. The hike in prices forced companies and governments to rethink overnight as market stability was shattered and organisations had to look for new ways to achieve the same ends as before. In 1979 Margaret Thatcher launched the market economy on an unsuspecting British workforce. The old rule book was being torn up, and people searched for ways to start compiling a new one. It was natural enough to turn to systems or models to help impose or restore order when there was little else to hang onto.

The models

Since the 1970s, models for formulating and implementing business strategy have grown in type and number to tackle the increasing complexity of the world around us.

We shall look at some of the major models which have influenced the answers to the key question concerning how to achieve competitive advantage:

How can we beat (outperform, nullify) the competition to produce goods at a price that the customer will pay?

These models generate activities that set down a method for examining internal resources and external opportunities or threats in order to make logical proposals for the future. They concentrate heavily on planning *processes* and require extensive information gathering and manipulation. They enjoyed their heyday in the 1960s and 1970s as the numbers of people involved in data gathering, manipulation and analysis grew to provide the raw material for the planners.

The Growth Model

This model focuses on one particular issue: growing the market by reducing production costs and increasing sales opportunities. Growing the market could involve concentrating on a specific type of customer, product or geographic scale.

Today, however, success stories are quickly observed by market competitors. Copying the competition becomes an industry habit as technology and quickly formed

partnerships and alliances make market entrance
affordable. It is hard to keep a growing market to yourself.

Porter's Five Forces Model

Michael Porter, in *Competitive Strategy*, argued that either
you become the lowest-cost producer in your industry to
achieve best performance or you differentiate your
products in such ways as to attract customers at premium
prices. In order to do this, the organisation has to select an
approach towards *customers, suppliers, substitutes,
competitors* and *new market entrants* depending on the
industry conditions at the time: fragmented, emerging,
mature, declining or global.

But it is not merely a question of collecting data in order to
position the organisation favourably in relation to these
forces. Porter argues that you have to break the rules and
change them to bring the organisation competitive
advantage:

- How can I reduce the influence of my customers and of
  my suppliers on my pricing?
- How can I limit the impact of substitutes – copies – on
  my product?
- How do I reduce rivalry in my industry, making
  competition unattractive, and nullify the impact of new
  industry entrants?

The logic of Porter's Five Forces Model has had a
considerable impact on formulating strategy in the 1980s
and 1990s. Such is the pace of industry and market change
that companies now have to compete not just on one but on
all five of Porter's forces. This process can be constrained
by the amount of information gathering, analysis and

interpretation that industry-, company- and market-watching require. We shall look further at Porter's Five Forces on Wednesday.

Growth by diversification/acquisition
Instead of going it alone, an organisation can buy success by acquiring another in order to gain entrance into new markets. Growth by diversification or acquisition gave rise to the formulation of analytical models that have enjoyed widespread application:

- The McKinsey/GE Matrix requires you to look closely at a company's market attractiveness in terms of its strategic position. It suggests acquisition and investment when an organisation is building a strong strategic position and market attractiveness is low. Divestment is recommended if the market becomes attractive to other players, and the organisation's competitive position is eroded.
- The Boston Consulting Group market growth/market share matrix became known as the Boston Box and attempted to indicate which businesses a company should invest in and which it should divest itself of. The model asks you to analyse which businesses have high market share and growth rates (Stars) and which are the opposites to these (Dogs). Moreover, if it has a high market share in a low-growth market, it is a Cash Cow which could yield significant, but short-term, gain; and the Question Marks are those businesses that have a low share in a high-growth market offering a questionable return on investment. See the diagram.

Figure 2. BCG market growth/market share matrix

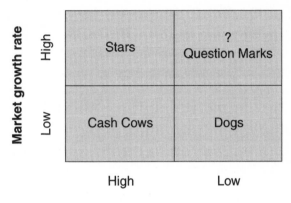

These models, and others, have proved useful for organisations wishing to diversify market risk. They still require, however, an accurate assessment of the prey's strengths and weaknesses, a good reading of which way the market will go and a probing estimate of the 'attractiveness' of the industry in which the prey operates.

Based on his Five Forces Model, Michael Porter established three critical questions to test whether an acquisition might be feasible:

1. *The attractiveness test*: is the industry 'attractive'? Is it one where there are only few rival products, competition is stable, and suppliers and customers have only moderate bargaining power?
2. *The cost-of-entry test*: is the cost of entry so high that a return on investment is at risk?

3. *The better-off test*: how can you demonstrate that either the acquirer or the acquired will gain competitive advantage from the link?

Growth by diversification means consistently monitoring the world outside the organisation. An equally vigilant eye has to be kept on the organisation's fitness for competition by looking at its own internal systems, processes and structure.

Traditional models

The Design School sets out a traditional top-down approach:

- Define the organisation's mission, develop a set of core values and principles, and define the vision
- Define the goals which are paramount to the mission and which will lead to achieving the vision and fit with values and principles
- Lay the plans to achieve the goals by scanning the market to identify attractive sectors, and assessing internal strengths and weaknesses
- Define the competitive advantage to be achieved
- Define the capability gaps and the resources needed to achieve the performance levels required
- Test the strategy against the mission, vision and values
- Break down the plan into achievable objectives and goals

The Resource-based Model looks at strategy from an internal point of view:

- Identify and classify the organisation's resources
- Appraise strengths and weaknesses
- Identify what it is that the organisation can do more efficiently or more effectively than competitors

- Appraise those resources and capabilities in terms of sustainable advantage – how easily will others be able to imitate them?
- Select the options which best exploit the organisational resources available to meet the external opportunities, and identify the resource gaps which need filling or strengthening

Porter's Value Chain

Porter's Value Chain focuses on the strengths and weaknesses at each stage of the supply chain to customers, and leads an organisation to examine what it is, and what it is not, good at.

The Value Chain looks at two different types of business activity: primary and secondary. Primary activities are mainly concerned with transforming raw materials into products and with delivery. These primary activities usually include:

- *inbound logistics*: materials handling, warehousing
- *operations*: turning raw materials into finished products
- *outbound logistics*: order processing and distribution
- *marketing and sales*: communication and pricing
- *service*: installation and after-sales.

Secondary activities support the primary ones and include:

- *procurement*: purchasing and supply
- *technology development*: know-how, procedures and skills
- *human resource management*: recruitment, appraisal, development and reward
- *firm infrastructure*: general management, quality, planning and finance.

To remain competitive and supply what customers want to buy, the organisation has to ensure that all these activities link together and fit, especially when some of them take place outside the organisation. A weakness in any part of the chain will affect the chain as a whole and impact negatively on competitiveness.

Core Competencies
The Model of Core Competencies, initially proposed by Gary Hamel and C. K. Prahalad, argues that an organisation can reach a position of competitiveness by analysing what it is that it does better than others. Looking at the organisation as a system of activities and building blocks – not as separate units of products and services – identifying core competencies means asking:

- How does activity X significantly improve the end product for the customer?
- Does activity X offer access to a range of applications and markets?
- What would happen to our competitiveness if we lost our strength in X?
- How difficult is it for others to imitate activity X and compete with us?

Success in core competencies means defining critical activities, and the skills that enable them, and investing in all of these to stretch and develop them.

Many organisations have not found this to be an easy process. And what happens if you get them wrong, or if the markets move away, or if you just hang onto them too long?

The McKinsey Seven-S Model

The Seven-S Model model suggests that the real value in an organisation is to be gained by looking at values other than the tangibles of capital, infrastructure and equipment. These 'softer' values are really about motivating the organisation's key resource – its people – to create a new competitive edge. The seven Ss are as shown in the diagram.

Figure 3.

They laid the basis for the empowering style of management which Peters and Waterman, both working for McKinsey at the time, popularised in their book *In Search of Excellence*.

How the models worked

As the importance of strategic planning grew, its information systems grew to feed it. These consisted principally of Management Information Systems (MISs) and of Decision Support Systems (DSSs).

Management Information Systems
These were run largely by middle and junior managers and
delivered large quantities of numerical data at regular times.
The data was probably factually correct, quite well organised,
but not too well analysed, and essentially historical. And
because there was so much of it, managers used to spend
large amounts of time looking for something salient.
Eventually, they would come up with something predictable,
gleaned tortuously from the computer print-out, or give up.

Decision Support Systems
These were based on the same data as the MIS above but
were slightly higher-level in that they did permit some
analysis that enabled the recipient to ask *What-if* questions.
They delivered useful results on occasions, especially in the
arena of spotting trends or patterns.

Because MISs and DSSs focused on historical data,
managers' preoccupations were also influenced in that
direction. Neither MISs nor DSSs could address the nature
of strategic – future or directional – issues.

The models and approaches above held muster when:

- forces driving society and business were relatively stable and predictable
- information gathered on past performance could be used with reliability for projecting the future
- strengths were not so easily copyable
- analysis of markets carried weight for some time into the future
- competition was either measurable or not a major problem.

In the later 1980s, confidence in these models of strategic planning fell and they were knocked off their pedestal. So what went wrong?

What changed?

In the 1970s and 1980s, the underlying business adage was: 'If it ain't broke, leave it alone'. The pedestal of strategic planning was lodged firmly in the upper echelons of the organisation, and planning – implementing strategy – was very much a top-down process. According to the formula, strategic planning was for the few to develop, for the middle to implement, and for the many to follow. It all started to go wrong when change speeded up.

In the 1980s, several factors led to organisational turmoil. The middle was knocked out of many organisations by cost cutting, outsourcing and downsizing. Others, small enough to be without much of a middle, found that their competitiveness was failing if they didn't adopt new working practices, such as empowering staff and using new technology. The world shrunk with more effective telecommunications, markets became global and cheap imports ate away previously secure market share. Market entry was made easier with a mobile workforce and new technology, and customers became more and more demanding as competition stimulated the thirst for something more and something different.

By 1990 – whether the organisation was small, medium or large – the rules of how to do business were changing faster than the ability to cope. This situation was further confused by the apparent conflict between key philosophies such as total quality and re-engineering – the former placing high value on people, the latter viewing them as disposable overheads.

To keep pace with volatility in the marketplace and gain competitive advantage, firms had to acquire new expertise, and reallocate resources on a grand scale in order to exploit new opportunities.

OUTPLACEMENT Inc

PEOPLE
ARE OUR GREATEST ASSET

Strategic planning no longer fitted the way markets worked. By the 1990s, the adage was switching to: 'If it ain't broke, break it anyway and start again'.

Why the models are no longer enough

The models still have a role to play in shaping our strategy but they don't give the whole picture. Models:

- can't predict the future with any certainty using information and experience from past conditions and circumstances – OK in times of stability but not in times of change;
- focus on products, markets and resources but not on generating values and capabilities for the future. What companies are good at today may not – and probably will not – be the critical success factors of tomorrow;
- become formulas for success concerned with maintaining the current position rather than frameworks for reflection, for questioning and for posing problems about where to go next;
- require an intensity of effort that locks the organisation into set processes and removes the flexibility to adapt and change direction.

What the models don't tell you

Models don't tell you about the unseen boundaries between organisations and the environments they work in, between management and subordinates, between planners and doers, between past and future, between those who formulate strategy and those who put it into action. Models don't tell you loud enough that they are not formulas to follow slavishly – or half-heartedly – but frameworks to stimulate thinking. They don't tell you:

- not to turn strategy over to an 'elite' team of experts who have the monopoly on strategic expertise by dint of their position, but who, in fact, may be far removed from customer activities and the buzz of new developments
- that strategy may be led by those who have the greatest incentive for preserving the status quo, not changing it, for doing things the same, not for doing different things
- that something imposed from above, however well planned and justifiable, will not work as well as something built from shared ownership
- to question information and experience from the past instead of assuming its reliability and validity
- not to hold onto a strategy too long, and when to drop it and change direction
- to do things differently and to do different things because it is difference that counts
- to experiment and try things out because nothing's for certain

Summary

Faced with a business environment where emerging technologies keep rewriting the rule book and markets grow and dissolve without consistency and predictability, we have to keep juggling several questions at the same time, questions such as:

- What is the organisation trying to achieve?
- What should it really be doing?
- Is there a difference between what it says and what it does?

Such is the pace of change, however, that these questions now have to be weighed not only against the organisation's resources and markets but also against new competition from outside its own industry.

By the mid-1990s, strategic planning as a discipline had lost its way because these questions had become too complex for the old models to provide a steer into an uncertain future. Just when organisations had lost confidence in strategic planning, new thinking emerged to turn much of the old on its head.

We look next at new approaches to strategy, bringing out some of the key points of the leading strategists, and some organisational strategies to illustrate them.

Strategists and strategies

The basis of such an approach is always to confront what is taken for granted in an industry or business with the simple question, Why? If, instead of accepting the first answer, one demands the reason for that and persists in asking 'Why?' four or five times in succession, one will certainly get to the guts of the issue, where fundamental bottlenecks and problems lie.

The Mind of the Strategist: the Art of Japanese Management, Kenichi Ohmae, McGraw-Hill, 1982

Today we are going take a look at strategists who have shaped the new wave of strategic thinking, and at examples of strategies from a variety of organisations. From this, we shall identify a number of key elements in the development of a successful strategy.

Strategy is a subject whose apparent complexity continues to fill endless numbers of books. The major writers on strategy, however, argue that there is no need for complexity, rather an understanding of some basic principles. These strategists are not just theorisers, but have taken some keen – and sometimes unpalatable – observations from companies which have succeeded in establishing strategies which work. Some key reading by each strategist is suggested for delving in deeper.

Today we look at:

- Strategists:
  - H. Igor Ansoff
  - Henry Mintzberg
  - Michael Porter
  - Gary Hamel
  - Richard Pascale

- Strategies with:
  - grated cheese
  - telephones
  - children
  - crime
  - strawberries

H. Igor Ansoff

H. Igor Ansoff has been called the 'first great thinker of strategy'. His book *Corporate Strategy*, published in 1965, had a great influence on strategy and planning in the 1970s and 1980s. He put forward a complex set of rules that focused on undertaking a detailed environmental analysis that required innumerable processes and decisions.

Although Ansoff's approach was suited to the relatively stable business environment of the 1960s and 1970s, it nonetheless produced success for only a few companies, and confusion for many. It led, quite simply, to the production of more and more plans that never got implemented.

In *Implanting Strategic Management,* Ansoff looked again at his approach – which he recognised caused 'paralysis by analysis' – and redefined his methodology for developing strategy to include greater flexibility for the ever-changing environment. Under the term Strategic Management – a broader concept than strategic planning – Ansoff proposed his Strategic Success Paradigm, which holds that there is no universal success formula for all firms.

He concluded that turbulence in the business environment is *the* key factor driving strategy. A firm needs to align the aggressiveness of its strategy to the pace and extent of change in the environment, and to ensure that its management has the capability and competence to match those changing conditions.

Key text

Ansoff, H. I. and McDonnell, E. J. (1990) *Implanting Strategic Management,* 2nd edn, New York: Prentice Hall.

Henry Mintzberg

Henry Mintzberg was an early proponent of the 'Design' school of strategy development, a 'top-down' approach to strategy that we covered yesterday.

Mintzberg has often derided the role of strategic planning in the strategy development process, favouring instead an informal approach to the analysis of an environment in which an organisation operates. Analysing the environment too closely, he feels, leads to strategies that are simply copies of those of competitors.

Mintzberg distinguishes strategy from planning:

- Planning concerns breaking down a goal or set of intentions into steps for implementation.
- Strategy is about synthesising the broader issues in order to come to that set of intentions.
- Planning is about formalising the steps to achieve a goal.
- Strategic thinking involves creativity and intuition to form a longer-term perspective for the organisation.
- Strategy means reinventing new ways of attracting customers, not just reordering the accepted products and services of the past. This requires an energising, committing style of management to engage participants in the reinvention process.

Mintzberg believes that strategic thinking – the ability to identify change when it occurs, to identify discontinuities and to recognise opportunities – is the key to successful strategy. Too much emphasis is placed on the rational, calculating – planning – approach, when in reality, strategies are usually born of the prevailing, even imminent, environmental conditions.

Key reference

Mintzberg, H. (1994) 'The fall and rise of strategic planning', *Harvard Business Review*, vol. 72 (1), pp. 107–114.

Michael Porter

Michael Porter played a key role in the development of strategy in the 1980s with his research on Competitive Advantage. He argued that the role of strategy was to ensure that the competitive forces facing the organisation were turned to its advantage by a process of differentiation from the competition. We noted Porter's Five Forces yesterday, and they play an important part in the analysis needed to kick-start the strategy process, which we look at tomorrow.

In the 1990s, Porter revisited his views on strategy to see how they held up as the millennium approached. He proposed that strategy does not emerge from schemes such as continuous improvement and reducing waste and duplication. These are sub-strategies or tactics. Strategy, he argues, is about:

- doing things differently or doing different things from those which rivals do, and being able to sustain that difference.
- making deliberate decisions on what *not* to do, because doing one thing well means *not* doing others. If the organisation does not take risks and make deliberate choices, it will compromise values and focus, and this may result in overtrading.

- how different processes fit together in the supply-production-delivery chain (the Value Chain – see yesterday). It is no good, for example, if you have a world-class production line and your distribution constantly lets you down. The *whole* matters more than its component *parts*, and is more difficult to copy.

Key reference

Porter, M. E. (1996) 'What is strategy?' *Harvard Business Review*, vol. 74 (6), pp. 61–78.

Gary Hamel

Read any of Gary Hamel's work and the word that stands out is 'revolution'. He believes that, to be successful in the modern organisational environment, strategy must not only be different from what has gone before but also be 'revolutionary'.

Hamel, like Mintzberg, argues that the strategic process has become too ritualistic, based on rules, and driven by the calendar. For strategy to be revolutionary, it must:

- be subversive by ignoring industry conventions, and aiming to be unique
- actively promote change, not simply be carried along with it
- let everyone have their voice, so that the new and young, as well as the tried and tested, are part of the process
- take risks, because we cannot predict the future with any certainty.

Hamel argues that it is usually senior managers who are the staunchest defenders of the status quo, that although they have the greatest experience, they also have the greatest investment in the past. He defines a new role for senior management which should:

- sponsor thinking about change and discontinuities
- consider all new ideas openly and honestly
- get involved in the learning process by casting off the mantle of omniscience
- foster intrapreneurship and participate in the creative process as team members, not just team leaders.

Key reference

Hamel, G. (1996) 'Strategy as revolution', *Harvard Business Review*, vol. 74 (4), pp. 69–82.

Richard Pascale

Management consultant and lecturer Richard Pascale uses the words 'transformation', 'breakthroughs', 'revitalisation' and 'reinvention' when he talks about strategy.

He proposes that organisations must undergo perpetual and 'radical' change in order to be successful. It is important, he advises, that organisations should not merely seek improvement but also create something that *isn't already there*. In other words they must become a totally different company, again and again. The failure of many companies to achieve this type of reinvention, Pascale believes, is due to the failure of leaders to take the inherent risks involved. In the 'new' organisational environment, firms that do not reinvent themselves will be overtaken by those that have boarded the 'reinvention rollercoaster'.

The path to reinvention requires a mix of so many different skills and abilities that it is not possible to rely solely on senior management. The burden of change must be placed on all of the organisation's employees if it is to succeed.

For Pascale, there are four vital indicators of an organisation's fitness for adaptability and strategic change:

1 power – do employees (believe that they) have the power to make things happen?
2 identity – do employees identify narrowly with their own section or unit, or with the organisation as a whole?
3 conflict – do people try to smooth over conflicts to safeguard the status quo, or do they try to confront and resolve them?
4 learning – how does the organisation handle new ideas?

To prepare an organisation for strategic change, Pascale argues that:

• people must not merely follow instructions but also apply their creative skills to improving and changing them
• encouraging straight talk is more painful than, but preferable to, organisational 'face-saving' and 'covering-up'
• setbacks are actually prime opportunities for learning and asking questions which cause discomfort such as 'Why are we doing this?' and 'What are we trying to achieve?'
• managing people means understanding the full picture – not just giving reward and recognition for a good job well done, but also development for future employability,

making work challenging and meaningful, and
encouraging employees to have a say in where the
organisation is going

Key reference

Pascale, R. et al. 'Changing the way we change' *Harvard
Business Review*, Nov–Dec 1997, pp. 127–138.

Strategies

Now that we have had a look at the some of the thinkers on
strategy, it is time to take a brief look at some strategies in
action.

Strategy with grated cheese
Dairyborn found a niche market supplying ready-grated
cheese to the catering industry, including Pizzaland and
Perfect Pizza. This produced massive growth and success
for Dairyborn. Then, its largest contract – Pizzaland –
switched to a rival supplier. Dairyborn had identified an
industry need and enjoyed dominant success, but it had no
strategy to face up to threat from a competitor. Two thirds
of Dairyborn's business was lost overnight.

The options also became obvious overnight: drift or
change. It took a step outside its established industry and
went straight to the food manufacturers themselves.

Dairyborn is now successful again, this time through
supplying cheese products to food manufacturers rather than
the catering industry. The experience of losing the Pizzaland

contract was instrumental in generating Dairyborn's strategy of differentiating itself from the competition.

Source: Bartram, P. (1998) 'The big cheese' *Director*, vol. 51 (6), January, pp. 32–36.

Strategy over the phone
Try to guess which organisation the following is describing and what service it is offering. It is taken from the organisation's promotional leaflet:

'_____ is the UK's leading 24 hour personal _____. Our personal service lets you take care of all your _____ needs by telephone, at a time and a place to suit you, 24 hours a day, 365 days a year.

Since the day we opened in 1989, we have never closed. Our friendly and professional _____ representatives are always on hand to assist you, which means that you never have to worry about catching us before closing time.'

First Direct is currently the most popular telephone banking service in the UK through innovative use of databases and automated telephone dialling, pushing back the boundaries of conventional service, and differentiating its services from those of the competition. This approach has made other banks wonder why they need their extensive – and expensive – high-street branch networks. While the major banks follow suit, it will be interesting to watch where First Direct goes next.

Strategy with children
Instead of tolerating a prevailing social trend on the part of youngsters to be disrespectful and disobedient, Horspath

Primary School, Oxfordshire, turned this situation on its head and went in the opposite direction by setting up a value system based on respect and positive attitude.

The teachers believed that if they encouraged children to adopt respectful behaviour and attitude, there would emerge an improved platform for developing them in the classroom.

They involved the children in everything the school does, such as improving the school playground and establishing reward and discipline systems. Achievement stickers are awarded for politeness, punctuality and tidiness, and this transferred into the academic arena as well where teachers concentrate on the basics, 'the three 'Rs', whichever subject is being taught. A pupil is as likely to be reprimanded for poor grammar in geography or history lessons as they are in English lessons.

In 1997, Horspath Primary School was in the middle of the county school rankings; in 1998 it was ranked in the top 45 schools in the country.

Horspath achieved success by going against the grain, turning what is 'conventionally acceptable' upside down, pushing out the boundaries of standard teaching wisdom, involving everyone and demonstrating to children that they can influence their environment by learning how to be responsible for it.

Source: Harris, P. (1998). 'Ringing in the changes that spell success' *Daily Mail*, Tuesday, 27 January, p. 19.

Strategy with crime – NYPD
When William Bratton took on the role of Police
Commissioner of New York, the city was a mess.
Muggings, theft, assaults, burglaries and crimes of violence
were all commonplace and people were leaving the city in
droves in search of some kind of quality of life.

The rising wave of crime was accompanied not by public
apathy but by inertia induced of fear and a lack of police
will to stop the rot. It was better for the police to stay out of
the way and keep their heads down: conventional wisdom
held that problems caused by society were impervious to
police intervention.

Bratton, however, believed that the police could have a significant impact on crime, that the police could control behaviour on the streets. He decided to fly in the face of conventional wisdom by speaking straight to the police force, telling them that he needed their help to take the city back from the criminals, that he wanted them to be assertive, that he didn't want them to look the other way, that he wanted them to be honest and to forget the old 'rules'. And he said he would back them up. If they had problems, he would see to their retraining; if they were crooked, he would break them.

Bratton wanted to set targets to bring crime down by 10 per cent in year 1, 15 per cent in year 2, then 25 per cent after that. But he was faced with the prevailing view that already as much as possible was being done. There emerged, however, some support which indicated that progress and improvement were possible as long as *everything* was changed, in every police department, from top to bottom.

Bratton adopted a number of schemes to tackle guns, drugs, and quality of life, even squeegee people who threateningly smeared windscreens at traffic lights.

In his first 6-monthly figures in 1995, murder was down by 31 per cent over the same period in 1994; robberies were down 22 per cent, burglaries down 18 per cent. Bratton was hailed as the Enforcer, the Architect of Zero Tolerance. What he did was, in fact, to go in the opposite direction, tear up the old rule book which said what should and should not be done, empower and support his workforce, and apply the law. Strikingly simple when explained on paper, not so easy to do in practice, and highly effective when seen through to the end.

Bratton left NYPD after an apparent clash of interests with the Mayor, but two years after his departure, the city is still recording spectacular success in reducing crime. Brooklyn recorded a full week without a murder – the first since records began. And Bratton is still hailed as the Magician who cleaned up New York.

Source: *Sunday Times News Review*, 22 March 1998, pp. 1–2, a review/extract from *Turnaround: How America's Top Cop Reversed the Crime Epidemic*, William Bratton, 1998.

Strategy with strawberries

The warmth of summer. The smell of ripe strawberries emerging from under their protective covering of leaves. The Pick Your Own sign attracts thousands to a pleasant ritual for a short season every July.

But is it really so pleasurable? The taste of strawberries is indisputable but many who pick their own also leave with aching legs, back and other assorted pains associated with uncomfortable bending and stooping.

Robert Symington of Seldom Seen Farm, Billesdon in Leicestershire has now changed all that for his customers. He has built a mile-stretch of homemade tables for his 2.5-acre site, which means that visitors can pick their strawberries at tabletop, or waste-height.

At present the tabletop technique can limit the crop to a few special brands, although the yield can be more prolific than at ground level. And there are extra benefits: 'tabling' enables a longer season as the berries ripen slower and later stretching the season for pickers into August. It also keeps the fruit safer from pests like mould.

Seldom Seen is the first strawberry farm in the East Midlands to experiment with tabling. The innovation has required an extra investment, but the strawberry-growers watch with interest to see if the results attract customers from further afield than usual, and how long it will be before others adopt the same practice.

Source: 'Tables enhance fruit quality' *Rutland Times*,
24 July 1998

The common factors

The mini case studies above are not one-off, remarkable achievements accomplished by the lucky few. Great strategies are all around us. Take a look at the daily newspaper and you will be able to point out two or three straight away, not just in the business world, but in every arena. Look at:

- the utility companies in the UK which have crossed industry boundaries to sell each others' goods
- New Labour's transformation into the party of middle England; notably, Gordon Brown's call for greater creativity and imagination in the reallocation of budget resources
- Flying Flowers, the Channel Islands-based home-delivery flower firm that can compete with the Interflora network
- Amazon Books on the Internet, which enriches the book-buying experience
- cricket, where Kerry Packer transformed interest in the game with his one-day circus

- snooker, which went from a seedy, back-room activity to an internationally televised sport

One to watch!

At the time of writing, Virgin Group has just announced plans to enter the arena of health and fitness clubs in a venture called Virgin Active. As with other diversification ventures such as Virgin Airways, Virgin Brides and Virgin Railways, the reasoning is quite simple: Virgin believes it can 'revolutionise' the industry by taking a different approach. Initially, 10 warehouse-style fitness centres will be set up, with more to come, offering low-cost and all-inclusive membership.

Virgin's strategy of entering industries and 'being different' has led to great success over the years, most notably in its airways and financial-products businesses. It will be interesting to watch how successful Virgin Active becomes, and importantly, how long it takes for another organisation to 'copy' the difference!

When we look at successful strategies, we can pick out a number of common factors:

- being different
- learning from the past, but focusing on the future
- changing continually
- pushing back the boundaries of the industry
- being innovative
- involving people from all areas of an organisation in the strategy process
- developing a flexible, continuing strategy

We have already mentioned the term 'competition' many times this week. If we take a second glance at the strategies above, we see that the protagonists – particularly the school and the police department – moved beyond competition to create new values for the organisation and for those taking part in implementing the new strategy.

Now is a good time to reflect on what we've learned today:

- Do you have a clear idea of what your strategy is?
- How does your organisation or department develop its strategy?
- Who is involved in the strategy process?
- Does your organisation cling to its industry's conventions?
- How different is your organisation from others in its area?
- How-fast changing is the environment in which your organisation operates?
- How different is your organisation today from two, five and ten years ago?

If the answers are unsettling, take heart from the cases above. Most organisations make mistakes, but the successful ones learn from them and change things.

Summary

Today we have looked at some writers on strategy, seen their ideas in practice and identified a number of key points in successful strategy.

For the next three days we are going to look at the key factors involved in developing a winning strategy. Tomorrow we will investigate the first of these: strategic analysis.

Strategic analysis

If your company comes to a plateau in earnings, take the time to look around and get your bearings. You may discover a whole new direction.

Up the Organization, Robert Townsend, Michael Joseph, 1970, p. 198.

Today we are going to look at ways in which we can make sense of our ever-changing environment. We are going to look at some of the 'old' tools of strategy to kick-start the strategic process.

We will cover:

- What is strategic analysis?
- Looking at the environment
- Looking at our organisation
- Looking at the competition
- Change trends

What is strategic analysis?

Effective analysis is about asking the right questions. It is important to keep in mind that the inferences we draw from information related to the past and present are precisely that – past and present – and not automatically valid for the future. Too often, we superimpose the past onto the future, assuming that things will be the same, or at least similar.

Remembering Ansoff's 'paralysis by analysis', it is useful to try to discover how we got where we are, and to have a clear understanding of what we did well, or badly, and why. But it becomes counter-productive to linger too long on conundra from the past, and dangerous to project a mirror-image of the past into the future. If it is over-exercised, analysis can switch straight into planning without thinking through the factors which make the difference. The future is not what it used to be.

With that caveat in mind, strategic analysis involves taking a look at the environment in which we operate. This means looking at:

- the wider environment for significant influences, and picking out the change and discontinuity factors
- our organisation, and examining its strengths and weaknesses
- our competition, and assessing opportunities and threats

Looking at the environment

A glimpse back at the strategists we mentioned on Tuesday reminds us that we ignore the environment and its changing permutations at our peril. Some may take coals to Newcastle and some sell sand to the Arabs, but they are few and far between.

PEST analysis is a technique that allows us to look at our environment by dividing it into four categories – see the diagram:

Figure 4. PEST analysis

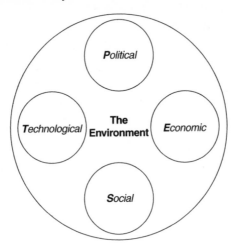

Here are some examples of PEST factors that have occurred in recent years, or are still continuing to roll out today:

- Political:
  - the shift towards capitalism and democracy in Eastern Europe
  - the recognition of the need to continuously 'read' the changing will of the people, instead of taking it for granted
  - moves towards Workfare in the USA and the UK

- Economic:
  - the opening up of new market potential in emerging economies
  - the departure of the UK from the European Exchange Rate Mechanism
  - the continued stance of the UK on EMU

- the impact of negative equity on the housing market – and other markets – in the UK
- a unified Germany
- Labour's handing over of the regulation of the UK interest rate to the Bank of England Monetary Policy Committee
- growing numbers of the elderly, and the impact of this on social security and pensions funding

- Social:
  - the growth of educated consumers seeking more choice, sophistication and differentiation
  - demographic shifts, with more women than men in the UK workforce
  - growing numbers of the elderly, and their impact on market forces
  - rising crime as an apparently 'socio-economic' phenomenon that we have to live with

- Technological:
  - the growth of the Internet and the advance of electronic communications
  - the affordability of computing in the home
  - the growth of cable and satellite TV and the service choices on offer
  - the millennium bug, with all its ramifications

Looking at our organisation

One of the best techniques for taking a good hard look at the organisation is a SWOT analysis. SWOTs can apply across diverse management functions and activities, but are particularly appropriate to the early stages of formulating strategy.

Performing a SWOT analysis means gaining a clear picture of the Strengths, Weaknesses, Opportunities, and Threats which made the organisation what it is. Although the SWOT should keep to an organisational focus, it necessarily incorporates reflection on, and analysis of, individual tasks, activities, people, functions and processes.

It is customary for the analysis to take account of internal resources and capabilities (strengths and weaknesses) and factors external to the organisation (opportunities and threats). So, whereas PEST analysis looks at the environment in which we operate, SWOT analysis uses its findings to assess how well placed our organisation is. (See the diagram.)

Figure 5. SWOT analysis

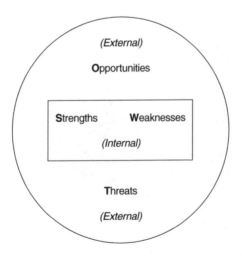

The effectiveness of SWOT as a means of analysis has recently been called into question because some of its practitioners:

- insist on the generation of long lists
- stop at description, instead of going on to analysis
- fail to prioritise

It is advisable to limit the exercise to the four or five most important factors affecting your organisation and focus thinking on whether these are really threats or opportunities (is the glass half empty or half full?). Do not concentrate on the marginal strengths or weaknesses of your organisation, but target the major areas.

Picking out strengths and weaknesses might go something like this:

Strengths	Weaknesses
Unique skills and competencies	Weak links in the Value Chain
Dominant product range	New product development drying up
Tradition of 'first to market'	Growth in staff turnover
Healthy balance sheet	Lack of 'spark' in the organisation
Creative teamworking	Growth of bureaucracy

As Peter Drucker said, asking the right questions is vital:

- What did we get right?
- What external factors enabled us to get it right at the time?
- What internal factors helped us to get it right?
- Are these factors likely to hold true in the future?
- What evidence do we have for suspecting this?

Looking at the competition

Michael Porter's 'Five Forces Model', that we referred to on Monday, can be used to identify the state of competition in an industry or market.

Figure 6.

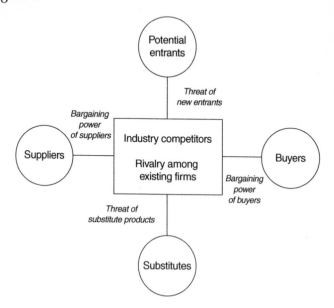

These five forces are:

1 *competitive rivalry*: competition is particularly strong when there are a large number of organisations competing in the same market solely on price and quality, and where differentiation between products and services is minimal.
   E.g. the clothing market, especially jeans.
2 *the power of suppliers*: suppliers can reduce an organisation's profits through higher charges, and can be particularly powerful when there is a small number of suppliers and the cost of changing suppliers is high.
   E.g. the 'old' utility industries in the UK.

3 *the power of buyers*: the power of buyers is increased
   when their number is small relative to the number of
   organisations within an industry. This force is inextricably
   linked to the following force below, i.e. the threat of
   substitutes.
   E.g. the ready availability (supply) of cheap, frozen food
   (e.g. burgers, chickens) but relatively few large-scale
   outlets (buyers – e.g. MacDonalds, Asda, Safeway)
4 *the threat of substitutes*: if a buyer can easily obtain a
   different product that meets the same need as an
   existing product, then the threat of substitution is high
   and an organisation is unable to raise prices too high.
   E.g. the advantages of e-mail over 'paper', although for
   many people the cost of switching to e-mail may make it
   sufficiently unattractive not to do so.
5 *the threat of potential entrants*: this covers the ease with
   which another company can gain entry into a market and
   so impact on an existing organisation. In some
   industries, the cost of entry in terms of capital
   requirements is so high as to deter potential entrants. In
   others, economies of scale prevent small operations from
   obtaining a foothold. Here, use of technology and
   temporary partnerships can rapidly change the shape of
   a market.
   E.g. the move by supermarkets into banking in the UK.

Effective strategies aim to swing these forces in favour of
the organisation. Porter's Five Forces Model highlights the
importance of 'being different'. By differentiating our
products and services, we can gain an advantage over the
competition, but this differentiation must be maintained if
competitors are not to catch up. Even so, this may still hold
only marginal validity for the future.

Trends differentiating the future from the past

There are a number of general trends that we should be aware of:

1 *Globalisation.* Organisations, of any size, no longer operate only in their own locality. Nor do their competitors. Many organisations start up with the sole intention of operating world-wide; they have been called 'born globals'. If global sounds too ambitious, it is nonetheless increasingly important not to confine yourself to too limited a locale.

2 *Technological advancement* – particularly in the areas of communication and information transfer. The explosion of the Internet in recent years is changing how businesses operate.

3 *Societal change.* A profound shift has occurred in the West from a manufacturing-based society to the information and knowledge society; organisations are now competing on knowledge and information. Your competitive advantage depends on what you know and how you put your knowledge to use.

4 *The organisation as a collection of stakeholders.* It is now accepted that organisations are much more than a group of employees. Progressive organisations involve their suppliers, customers and shareholders, as well as their employees, in their strategy. These groups are the ones who have a 'stake' in the organisation, hence the term 'stakeholders'.

5 *The reliance on innovation for success.* Organisations that do 'the same old thing' while the environment around them changes are on course for failure. Innovation, doing new and different things, is what provides an

organisation with an advantage over its competitors. Tom Peters has coined the phrase 'Get innovative or get dead'!

6 *The nature of competition.* No longer do industry giants have an unchallenged monopoly. Small companies such as Netscape and Amazon Books can now compete directly with the major industry players.

7 *A more diverse workforce* – including older workers, women and those from ethnic minorities. Diversity both impacts on, and enriches, the working practices and services that organisations can offer.

8 *Changing organisational structure.* Where organisations use outsourcing, empowerment and communications technologies, they can be more flexible and responsive to market opportunities.

9 *The need for lifelong learning* – to ensure skills change with the requirements of the environment. It has been said that learning is the real key to competitive advantage in the future.

10 *The increasing speed of change* – and it's getting quicker.

Don't dwell in the past

Using your findings from brief PEST and SWOT analyses, and using Porter's Five Forces to find out the most important forces impacting on your organisation, try to address the following:

- What changes are happening in today's markets?
- In which market areas do you have the best chance of success?

- How are customers' attitudes and demands changing?
- Will the critical success factors of today hold good for tomorrow?
- How well do you think your organisation's current strategy will fit into the future?
- How quickly could your organisation change to take advantage of opportunities and defend against threats?
- Do you have the flexibility to change direction rapidly?
- How is technology changing what you do?
- What key skills do you need to develop?
- Do you have a learning workforce, or an obedient one?

Summary

Today we have taken a look at some tools that can enable us to identify the changes that are taking place in our environment and help to tackle the questions above. But analysis alone doesn't make a great strategy. We can recognise one when we see one, but how do we create one?

Tomorrow we look at strategic thinking.

Strategic thinking

> *If you want to build a ship, don't drum up people together to collect wood and don't assign them tasks of work, but rather teach them to long for the endless immensity of the sea.*
>
> Anon.

If strategic analysis is about where you have been in the past and how you have arrived at the present, it is not necessarily about how to take you into the future. Where the organisation is going in the future depends more on the capability for strategic thinking.

What is strategic thinking? How can the organisation create a climate where strategic thinking occurs naturally instead of being ignored, repressed or thought of as something that only others can do?

Today we shall look at:

- looking for something different
- what strategic thinking involves
- harnessing conflict
- getting involved
- finding time
- sharing information
- asking the right questions

Looking for something different

Continuous efforts to shave costs have resulted in increased efficiencies that have improved quality for the customer. In a period of intense competition, however, operational efficiencies alone are not enough. Strategy is about doing different things in different ways, about taking a different path from the mainstream, about standing out from the crowd. Cloning competitors' products works well when profits can be made from margins of improvement, but there comes a day when improvement runs out of steam because you have ultimately milked every improvement conceivable.

Looking for something different means making a case for continuous change because customers are always changing habits, preferences, needs and wants. As soon as you find them, they move on. Research and observation show that this is happening for the majority of customers over shorter periods of time and that the pace of change is speeding up all the time.

Looking for something different means going against the grain of convention – such as we saw on Tuesday – with strategies that break the mould. Doing different things means recognising what customers value, getting the customer involved to tailor and personalise products to stand out from the norm, and passing on visible benefits. It also means leading the customer to make discoveries and try things out. This is very much the case with products born of new technology: there was no great public outcry for mobile phones, for mouse-click technology or for CD-ROMs. There was, rather, a risk, along with intuitive foresight that this was where the market could go.

AND YOU'LL BE ABLE TO TALK TO PEOPLE HUNDREDS OF MILES AWAY.

Strategy can be based on method but it can also be emerging and dynamic. It can be adaptive but it can also be revolutionary. It can mean changing or developing products at the height of their success, before competitive watchers clone the product and eat away at market share. It means that imagination and creativity are given greater scope when it comes to trying things out.

What strategic thinking involves

Thinking strategically is not something you can turn on or off like a tap, nor is it something that can be set aside for an annual meeting. It is something that should take place continuously, perhaps in formal sessions, perhaps between individuals who have struck up a relationship which carries them outside the confines of day-to-day operations.

Strategic thinking is not just about solving problems. Problem-solving is related to norms and standards;

strategic thinking is about breaking the rules to write new ones. It is more about *creating* problems and setting challenges which take the organisation down a new path. Strategic thinking has a number of characteristics. It means:

1 casting off a risk-averse culture where things that are 'out of line' or not really 'our style' are not rejected out of hand or dismissed as the ramblings of a crank, but are positively assessed. It means allowing people to get things wrong and not always be 'held to account' when initiative or inspiration do not immediately meet bottom-line requirements;

2 being able to kick around ideas in a climate where colleagues and others have the freedom to explore new ideas, and where omniscience at the top is replaced with a recognition that no one individual or set of individuals can know it all. This means information sharing and communication on a different scale from the past. It means encouraging cross-functional conversations to get dialogue going in place of linear thinking which 'departments' and partitions tend to foster;

3 recognising that the same old voices will probably come up with the same old thinking, that those voices were once fresh and new, and now the strategic process needs invigorating again with new voices – the young, customers, potential customers and suppliers with a different perspective;

4 releasing some desires and passions to make that difference happen, and that means letting the patterns and rhythms of the right brain have their say along with the logic, order and calculation of the left. Research has shown that the left side of the brain is good at analysing,

using reason and putting ideas into words, while the right, on the other hand, is the more creative, intuitive side that sees the 'whole' picture;

OKAY, LET'S THINK THAT ONE OUT!

THIS IS HOW I SEE IT

LANGUAGE | WHOLES
LOGIC | PATTERNS
ANALYSIS | INTUITIONS

5 nurturing creativity and new patterns of thinking through techniques of brainstorming, where people become involved in spontaneous, open-ended discussions in search of new ideas;
6 challenging old assumptions and suspending the judgement that new ideas don't appear to fit. Looking for new ideas means breaking away from the old 'fit'. This is very much akin to Edward de Bono's lateral thinking which is *concerned with breaking out of the concept prisons of old ideas. This leads to changes in attitude and approach; to looking in a different way at things which have always been looked at in the same way. Liberation from old ideas and stimulation of new ones are twin aspects of lateral thinking.*

Lateral Thinking: a Textbook of Creativity,
Edward de Bono, Ward Lock Educational, 1970, p. 11.

7 assimilating the notion that individual learning and development are at the heart of strategy, and that this may mean that the organisation reinvents its approach to individuals, how they are 'expected' to 'behave', how they manage their time, even how they are rewarded;

8 trying out new things. But that means conflict because some people will always prefer to stay with the way things are.

Harnessing conflict

Creating a climate conducive to the exchange of ideas and the sharing of information means building relationships which are founded on mutual respect, empathy and trust, rather than on position, status and authority. It means taking time to get involved in conversations and listening to what others have to say instead of wishing to dominate.

We have learned that the way to manage interpersonal conflict is to listen, treat the problem with respect, withhold opinions and 'solutions' and get people to come up with their own. Factors to be avoided include:

- the notion of knowledge as a privilege of position – the days when only certain individuals have the monopoly on intelligence, expertise and vision are long gone; now they are to manage it, nurture it, harness it and exploit it instead of own it by dint of seniority;
- ignoring undercurrents or sweeping differences under the carpet so that you can carry on as before;
- ignoring 'off the wall' contributions, which are, in fact, all the more valuable because they are different and require alternative treatment. Much 'blue sky' conversation may

happen, perhaps, but it is often dismissed as idle
rambling or the outpouring of tacit rebellion;
- taking a shorter-term view of things 'that don't gel':
  - of compromise and conciliation that lock you back into
    the status quo
  - of paradoxes and contradictions that rattle against the
    norm
  - of organisational protection and face-saving that will
    probably see you keep on making the same old
    mistakes in the future;
- short-term projects which may seem exciting on the
  surface but actually divert attention from longer-term goals.

Getting involved

So how does real involvement happen? Not just token
consultation when minds are already made up, positions
are being defended, and change is viewed as a threat – not
a challenge to keep the organisation ticking. There are a
number of ways to build a climate of involvement:

1 Getting out of the office and walking about to build
   contacts and relationships and to find out what is really
   going on – not just what the monthly reports tell you – is
   important.
2 Some organisations have found that strategic away-days
   or weekend retreats *do* work. But they have to include a
   mix of key stakeholders – not just the corporate planning
   team. Participants go along to listen with openness and
   honesty, and to exchange thoughts and ideas which
   some might find uncomfortable. Making people
   uncomfortable is central when change is overdue. Some

parts of the organisation may have to recognise that what they thought they do so well may not be quite the view held by others.

3 Getting involved means *making* suggestion schemes work by planning out what will happen in terms of reward and feedback to the suggester, rather than just placing a box in Reception and flipping through it once a quarter. Strategic thinking means getting others involved by spreading strategy wide, inside and outside the organisation.

4 On an individual basis, it means making teams work, not by drawing people together from different departments or functions and giving them something extra to do – the 'project' – but rather by understanding what each can contribute towards shared goals.

5 It means understanding the basis for trust in the organisation. Trust works OK when individuals begin to rely on each other in a continuing working context, but when they only meet now and again, it is not so easy. In some cultures, trust can hinge on a person's dependability to deliver on promises and meet deadlines; in others, renegotiating timetables is not seen as critical. In some cultures, a pervasive air of disagreement and suspicion leads people to get hung up on minor points and become entrenched in fixed positions; in others, respect and sincerity are enhanced by 'straight talk' and eye-to-eye contact. In others again, direct eye contact is an indicator of anger or aggression.

6 Getting people involved also means taking time to let them feel their way. It may be time-consuming at the beginning, but it is better to start slowly, in tune with the adaptability of those concerned, rather than blow things apart by going too fast.

Finding time

So how do we bring about these changes to the way we work in order to create 'thinking' time?

Unfortunately, there are no magic formulas for time management. Most of us are relatively poor at self-discipline and dominated by day-to-day problems that send us crashing from one interruption to another, forgetting what is important and driven by the urgent. The confusion between the urgent and the important can create conflicts for the individual. But it is the urgent which envelops us in firefighting and problem-solving because things have to be 'put right' before all else. When the urgent dominates, it also tends to reinforce the status quo.

How often do we set aside time for:

- planning development activities
- coaching and counselling colleagues
- building relationships
- getting honest feedback on the way we work
- concentrating on self-development
- taking time out to read or explore pastures anew?

These are activities – we say – which are important, but we tend to postpone them, push them back, or carry them out far too infrequently. Yet these are the *very activities which can change the way we work*. Changing priorities is not about cramming more into an overcrowded day; it is more about making a strategic reassessment of what can really help to change the focus of the workplace, and getting to grips with activities which are too often postponed.

Sharing information

Information and knowledge sharing is now recognised to be the key factor in an organisation's efforts to compete in the marketplace. Creativity – the ability to come up with ideas that work – is *the* asset which has distinguished the rule makers from the followers.

Successful organisations have moved away from the past when information meant personal power. Information hoarders have been bypassed by open systems of communication such as Intranets which become the first and last resort for depositing and finding information within the organisation.

Sharing ideas, keeping others abreast of progress, projects and developments, making information available to those who might pick it up and run with it are all seen as key components of the organisation's developing as a knowledge organism.

Asking the right questions

Asking the right questions means getting down to a thorough health check of the *key factors* you have to get right if you are to cope with strategic change:

- *Strategy*: does everyone know what they are doing and why? Do they know how they contribute to the strategic objectives of the organisation?
- *Leadership*: does the leader set an example, act as a role model and foster learning and development?
- *Customers*: does everyone have a good understanding of their needs and expectations? Are we going to try to steer them, outguess them or just hope for the best?
- *People*: are our people developing, innovative and responsible? Do people think naturally about what's coming next? Or will the next change be met with the same old shock and horror?
- *Control*: do measurement and procedural control stifle creativity?
- *Integration*: do we have a business of people in separate boxes or do we mix across areas, functions and responsibilities?
- *Processes*: which are the key activities and processes which give us our strength?
- *Results*: is our focus entirely on the short-term bottom line, or are we looking 3–5 years ahead and investing for it?

Asking the right questions also means getting the imagination to work on the key strategic drivers that affect the way the marketplace works. It can often mean leading customers rather than following them. Focusing on the future does not mean forecasting, predicting or working out a plan – usually, such attempts end in ignominy. It does, however, mean accepting that change will probably take us all onto a new playing field.

Strategy today means tackling the questions that will shape a tomorrow where, sooner or later, perhaps:

- over 50 per cent of homes are linked up to the Internet and/or Cable TV
- cyber-homes look after their residents, with one computer controlling lighting, security, heating and appliances, and righting malfunctions while another provides online banking, shopping, recreation and education services

- businesses operate 24-hour services as a norm through virtual link-ups and call-centres
- fossil fuels have become so expensive that there are fewer cars on the road than in the 1950s
- climate changes have shifted the Gulf Stream to create hotter summers but colder winters in Northern Europe

Blue-sky perhaps, but strategically these pictures – or others – of the future will shape what business is done and how.

If one key to competitive advantage means being first, then we need to take the simple questions and project them three, five years forward:

- Who will be our customers in the future?
- What will be their concerns and priorities?
- What kind of lifestyle will they have or expect?
- How shall we get close to them?
- What will be customer preferences for getting access to products and services?
- What will be the major channels for reaching customers?
- How can we adapt or radically transform our products and services for future requirements?
- What should we do to exploit information, develop knowledge and invest in skills?

Summary

Today we have looked at some of the factors involved in strategic thinking, which can break us away from the mould of conventional routine and attitude. Tomorrow we look at how to take this forward by turning the strategy in development into action.

From strategy to action

You're questioning my judgment, Lewis. I can't have that!

From the TV series *Inspector Morse*, by Colin Dexter

Turning strategy into action means planning, and planning means creating objectives which are achievable and challenging and earn the commitment of those who are to carry them out. For effective planning, we need:

- an approach which can deliver the strategy
- a style of leadership to produce the changes to drive the strategy forward
- a framework for change that breaks down resistance and obstacles and creates a receptivity to the direction that the organisation has chosen
- effective teamworking to put the changes into action

Today we shall look at:

- a planning approach
- leadership
- a framework for change
- teamworking

A planning approach

Planning is essentially about turning the strategy into action, deciding what the objectives are, who will do them, when and how. Identifying the objectives is a process – like the generation and regeneration of strategy itself – which requires discussion, co-ordination and people to buy into them if the objectives are to be made to work.

Planning will usually involve most, or all, of the following steps:

1 Define and agree the overall strategy.
2 Identify longer- and, subsequently, shorter-term objectives.
3 Assess the gap between current performance and that required to tackle the objectives.
4 Determine resource and skill reallocation to bridge the gap, or the level of new skills and resources required, or both.
5 Work out a timetable of key targets or milestones which have to be achieved if the plan is to progress.
6 Attempt to assess where the real problems lay in steps 3–5.
7 Develop the sub-strategies, or tactics, for implementation, including contingencies to overcome step 6.

Each objective will probably have its own portfolio of problems and will need tactics to tackle them, and each will probably require its own project management. If the people involved in the 'doing' have been involved in the formulation of the strategy and the subsequent planning stages, step 6 above becomes more natural, instead of a minefield. The change process will inevitably involve a transition from where you are to where you want to be. This will require the process to be tackled as a whole – not piecemeal – along with teamwork and good leadership.

The leadership conundrum

Clichés on leadership abound: 'Leaders are born not made', 'Cometh the hour cometh the man', etc. etc.

Whether or not leaders can be 'made', a style of leadership has emerged in the competitive marketplace that is in tune with people who challenge and question rather than merely accept and follow.

Is a leader one who:

- challenges assumptions and breaks the rules?
- expects the best from their people?
- orchestrates, facilitates and co-ordinates?
- gets their hands dirty?

Or is a leader someone:

- who focuses on the bottom line?
- to whom you can happily take all your problems?
- who is a hero with all the answers?

Trying to get changes through with a leader who is 'a hero with all the answers' usually ends in inertia and tears. On the other hand, having a leader who is so remote as to appear uninterested leads to confusion, and a loss of that valuable sense of 'belonging'.

Leaders seem to be people who can be strong when required, and who set the framework for moving forward. But they also know when to step back, let others have their head, and yet continue to guide and steer in the right direction.

Leadership is more about releasing power and harnessing conflict than control. It is about making the change agenda proactive instead of reactive. This is what John Harvey-Jones, former CEO of ICI and now TV troubleshooter, had to say about his style of leadership:

I'm just a hired hack – a professional manager, I'm proud of that – I'm not a proprietor, not dominant. I lead by example and persuasion and a hell of a lot of hard work. Not on the basis of power or authority. My skills are to help a large number of people to release their energies and focus themselves. It is switching on a lot of people and helping them achieve a common aim. People only do things they are convinced about. One has to create conditions in which people want to give of their best.

> Sir John Harvey-Jones in *Great Leaders*,
> John Adair, Talbot Adair Press, 1989, p. 221

A framework for change

Throughout the week, we have talked of the inevitability of change and how it causes problems. We have said that strategy means creating problems and not merely sweeping everything ugly under the carpet.

We now take a more in-depth look at how change works, or how it can be made to have a greater chance of success. We start by looking at the main reasons why change fails.

Why change fails
First, there is the way it is introduced, where the poorly delivered, surprise announcement creates a sense of threat, loss and a fear of the unknown. Those who introduce the change are probably not those who will be carrying it out. The reasons behind the fears might lie in the upper levels of the organisation:

- a lack of top-level understanding of what the business is about in operational terms
- a lack of thorough planning, preparation and listening
- a lack of direction (not directiveness) and motivation
- an old-fashioned attitude towards bottom-up suggestions
- a lack of real vision

There could well be a misconception of the scale and impact of change where:

- resource shortcomings are overlooked
- routine workloads are not accounted for
- goals are too far away
- the counting/measuring culture dominates
- training is overlooked

All combine to create a doomed start to the change process.

There is also the legacy of previous changes or failures to take into consideration, such as misreading the organisational culture:

- a prevailing attitude of 'We don't do things like that around here'
- organisational face-saving where root causes to problems are unspoken of or shielded because, if they surface, the upheaval will be too unsettling

Some of the (apparently) simpler questions will have been forgotten by those introducing and those implementing change, questions such as:

- How will staff react to this?
- Will this take them by surprise?
- What steps have we taken to minimise surprise?
- Have we underestimated staff?

In some organisations, these questions are simply not asked; in others they are used to benefit the change process.

The change agenda
The change agenda has its roots in the strategic analysis process which we looked at on Wednesday, and the strategic thinking process covered yesterday where we go for strategies that differentiate us from the others.

Change means not only fostering innovation and getting to grips with strategic uncertainties, but also keeping a sense of balance – control *and* flexibility, constancy *not* rigidity. It also means developing the right culture, something which cannot be achieved overnight.

A successful change environment means:

1 *building commitment:*
   - sharing information as widely as possible

- allowing for suggestions, input and differences from widespread participation
- breaking changes into manageable chunks and minimising surprises
- making standards and requirements clear
- being honest about the downside

2 *developing a culture that supports change:*
- recognising prevalent value systems
- creating a blame-free culture of empowerment, and pushing down decision-making – but clarifying decision boundaries
- breaking down departmental barriers
- designing challenging jobs
- freeing time for risk and innovation
- focusing on the interests of *all* stakeholders

3 *getting the people right:*
- recognising staff needs, and dealing with conflict positively
- being directional without being directive
- involving everyone
- earning commitment and trust
- developing relationships
- understanding how teams work
- recognising one's limits and others' strengths.

Rules for managing change

1 *Get the focus right.* Read a book which tackles change management; for example, John Kotter's *A Force for Change* or Rosabeth Moss Kanter's *The Change Masters*. Reading a book will take a day or two, whereas

the change process itself that you are trying to manage will take longer and cost a lot more – especially if you get it wrong.

2 *Think the change through.* Ask what kind of change may be involved from a broader perspective. Will it affect job content and responsibility, lead to new – unknown – tasks, new methods of working, new skills, new relationships, threats to security, new training, retraining? Will it be something on a broader scale that involves rethinking what the purpose of the organisation is or should be?

3 *Carry out an organisational audit.* This involves both present and future assumptions about:
   • key functions and systems
   • customer expectations
   • core skills and competencies

4 *Set up a team of stakeholders.* It is advisable not to include top management, but top management sponsorship would be a benefit. The team will include

the key people involved in designing and delivering the service, as well as those receiving it. They will also be responsible for defining and disseminating the benefits of the change.

5 *Create a sense of purpose and urgency to tackle real problems which have prevented progress in the past.*
   - Ask what and who is preventing progress and who can really help in unblocking it
   - Think of breaking the code of silence that supports organisational protectionism and maintains the status quo
   - Loosen up control parameters to enable more creativity and put differences and tension to work positively

6 *Be prepared for conflict.* Change usually brings about conflict of one kind or another, simply because people have different views and reactions. Try to get conflict to surface rather than let it fester; try to tackle it by dissecting and analysing it with those who are experiencing it. Often enough, conflict can be put to positive work through open discussion and clarification.

7 *Be willing to negotiate.* When conflict cannot be resolved through improved explanation and discussion, you will have to negotiate and persuade. This means avoiding entrenched positions, and working out how to shift others from theirs. It means getting to an agreed 'yes' without either side winning or losing face.

8 *Build in the capability for learning.* Creating goals and plans that everyone subscribes to means that everyone can gain. Turn learning into something that people want to buy into – instead of it being perceived as a chore –

where they can feel the 'buzz' of discovery and the involvement in new developments.

9 *Plan how to get commitment throughout the change process*
  - Plan how to prepare employees permanently – not incrementally – for change
  - Plan how to sell the advantages of the change proposal meaningfully and concisely
  - Plan how to acknowledge any downsides openly and honestly
  - Plan how to win over resistance and convert the stagnant into the active, how to create effective ownership
  - Allow for things to go wrong

10 *Go for specific objectives*. These are not quick fixes but early wins which demonstrate the benefits of the change. Think who can best help to achieve that early success which demonstrates that change is working.

Teamworking

Teams are not the same as other groups, and they need to be planned, built and maintained, and dissolved when their job is done. They need a mix of talents and skills that may not necessarily be drawn from one cohesive unit or section alone. What unites them is a common purpose and their potential contribution to achieving it.

At the outset, you have to decide if you really need a team – in some cases an individual working alone may achieve a task more effectively than a group. The benefit of a team is a mix of different capabilities, including personal and technical skills.

You need to think about how you want the team to operate in terms of:

- co-ordinating individuals' efforts in tackling complex tasks
- making the most of individuals' strengths
- raising and maintaining motivation
- encouraging team members to spark ideas off each other
- bringing about commitment and ownership of the task

To succeed with this, you will need to establish the ground rules. There will be a need for honest and open communication so that everyone – especially those with minority views – can say what they think without fear of put-down or ridicule. Include yourself – the team-leader – as a team member who passes on the leadership of the team when specific skills are required. This will also require the allocation of responsibilities and working out how to measure progress and report it.

Teamworking tips

1 Change is impossible without agreement and commitment.
2 Realistic timetables are vital, as unlearning may have to take place first.
3 Teambuilding will probably increase individual workloads.
4 Development is basically self-regulated, and domination undermines individual and team progress.
5 People cannot be forced into attitude changes.
6 Stick to the agenda but be open to new and different ideas.

7 Admit when you are wrong, and learn from mistakes – if you are right all the time, you are probably not developing.
8 You can't necessarily motivate people; you can only create the right conditions for motivation to happen.

Summary

Planning is a combination of turning the strategy into objectives, setting down a process to achieve them, recognising that this means preparation on an organisational scale and managing the obstacles anticipated with the best resources of leadership and teamworking available.

Tomorrow we bring together many of the themes covered in the week and summarise the key factors for formulating strategy.

Formulating strategy

> *This book does not project trends; it examines discontinuities.*
> *It does not forecast tomorrow…It asks instead: 'What do we*
> *have to tackle today to make tomorrow?'*
>
> Peter Drucker in the preface to
> *The Age of Discontinuity*, Heinemann, 1969.

Today we are going to summarise the key points of the
week and highlight the key points of strategy:

- Reviewing the week
- Seven thought-starters
- The end, or the beginning

Reviewing the week

We began the week by defining strategy as: *what we want to do,
what we want our organisation to be and where we want it to go.*

Strategy differs from 'tactics' and 'planning' by providing
an organisation with a framework for it to:

- understand its position in the changing marketplace
- move forward with a sense of purpose and urgency
- focus on the key issues of customers and markets,
  and on the skills needed to deliver to those
  customers and markets

Next, we looked at how strategy got bogged down in a
complexity of models, and highlighted the reasons why
these models were unable to stand up to the rigours of the
late 1980s and 1990s:

- Models can't predict the future with any certainty using information and experience from past conditions.
- Models focus on products, markets and resources but not on generating values and capabilities for the future. What companies are good at today may not and probably will not – be what they need to be good at tomorrow.
- Models become preoccupied with maintaining the current position rather than with frameworks for reflection and questioning where to go next.
- Models require an intensity of effort that locks the organisation into set processes and removes the flexibility to adapt and change direction.

On Tuesday we looked at some of the acknowledged strategists whose message focused on:

- being flexible to adapt to the changing environment
- reinventing new ways of attracting and retaining customers
- doing things differently and doing different things to stand out from the pack
- rejecting industry conventions and boundaries, by thinking creatively and acting boldly
- involving everyone within the organisation in the strategy process, because corporate planners hold no monopoly over good ideas
- preparing for strategic change by asking uncomfortable questions about traditional practices and encouraging straight talking rather than 'covering up' or 'saving face'

On Wednesday, we attempted to make sense of our ever-changing environment by looking at SWOT and PEST analyses and the trends that are changing the way we do business. We moved on from an analysis of the past and present by asking the key questions which can help to determine an organisation's future direction:

- What changes are happening in today's markets?
- How well do you think your organisation's current strategy will fit into the future?
- How quickly could your organisation change to take advantage of opportunities and defend against threats?
- In which market areas do you have the best chance of success?
- What is happening to customers' attitudes and demands?
- Will the critical success factors of today hold good for tomorrow?
- What key skills do you need to develop?

On Thursday we looked at the key factor in formulating strategy: strategic thinking; creating problems and setting challenges which take the organisation down a different path from that of the past. This means:

- casting off a risk-averse culture and replacing it with a culture where new ideas are encouraged and positively assessed
- working from the future back to the present, rather than looking forward from the past
- reinventing the organisation where necessary so that individual learning and development are at the heart of strategy, and the rewards for individuals are geared to it

On Friday we took a brief look at how we could move our strategy into action by setting down change guidelines to provide the strategy with the best chance of success. This meant tackling the main factors in preparing the ground of moving from A to B, how certain styles of leadership can help – and others hinder – and how approaches to teamwork need to be set up before the detailed planning process can begin.

Seven thought-starters

The development of strategy is an art rather than a science, and as such there can really be no set rules. We stress some key factors to help you get started in ensuring that your organisation's strategy stands a chance of success:

1 *Seriously question, if not totally ignore, tradition.* Think outside of the 'box' within which your organisation operates. No organisation can afford to believe that competition or changes will come from solely within its own industry, or that a small firm cannot overturn the largest. Who would have thought – a few years ago – that supermarkets would move into the banking sector in

the UK? The opportunities and threats for organisations in the present environment are limited only by an organisation's ability to break industry traditions, conventions and boundaries. This means keeping a sharp eye on surroundings and asking unwelcome questions which can cause conflict.

2 *Involve everyone – follow a top-down and bottom-up approach to strategy*. None of us has a monopoly on good ideas, and no-one can predict the future with any accuracy. Successful organisations focus on the customer, yet it is most often the people furthest away from the customer who develop strategy. Beware of the seven deadly sins of comfort, complacency, conceit, convention, following fads without strategic purpose, overreliance on experience, and confusing computer-generated data with knowledge.

3 *Avoid 'paralysis by analysis'*. Spending too much time and effort trying to develop the most accurate and

detailed picture of today does not enable us to get in position to determine the future, or *make tomorrow*, as Drucker says. Look ahead, but not blindly nor obsessively; remember the saying 'If you keep your eyes on the distant horizon, you may trip over a stone', but don't just look at the stones.

4 *Encourage and foster innovation and creativity throughout the organisation.* Doing something different requires the need for innovation within an organisation. To help foster innovation, an organisation must ensure that risks are allowed and that employees who take them with the goal of improving organisational success are not blamed if they don't work out. Strike a balance between accountability on the one hand and risk on the other. Ensure that staff have an opportunity for development *and* to make their contribution.

5 *Go for balance.* There has to be a balance between getting things done (maintenance) and tackling new things (progress), and a balance between focus on the quarterly returns and an exciting direction for the future.

6 *Embrace conflict as unavoidable in strategic change – and plan to exploit it.* Change can invoke fear; for change to be successful, conflict has to be managed and used to advantage, not ignored.

7 *Remember that strategy never stops.* Organisations can no longer afford to lock themselves into 5- or 10-year strategic plans. Strategy has to be *continually* modified if an organisation is to shape its own direction. The perfect strategy is rarely achieved as a straight line; learning from mistakes will help ensure that it becomes possible.

The end, or the beginning

For some organisations, this week's advice will seem unachievable. We hear cries of 'We can't do that' or 'We don't work like that'. In which case, it probably won't work, because strategy is largely a question of attitude, will and trust.

There are three types of organisation:

1 *The Movers*: organisations which continually change to meet the needs of their environment and constantly innovate to find new ways of delighting their customers and differentiating themselves from the competition. These organisations take a proactive approach to change and innovation, and put learning at the centre of their development.
2 *The Watchers*: organisations that play 'catch-up' with the competition. These organisations wait and see what impact changes in the environment have, and then copy the successes of other organisations. Such organisations will remain in a precarious position by being reactive to change and are more likely to become failures than successes.
3 *The Short-lived*: organisations that do not change and innovate, and lose out.

It is a salutary thought that the average life-span of a small business is 3–5 years, even more eye-popping that for a large one it's about 30 years. A company may be strong (if a household name, it appears part of the permanent landscape), yet it can disappear very quickly. Current success holds very little sway over future success. Strategy does.

Further *Successful Business in a Week* **titles from Hodder & Stoughton and the Institute of Management all at £6.99**

All Hodder & Stoughton books are available from your local bookshop or can be ordered direct from the publisher. Just tick the titles you want and fill in the form below. Prices and availability subject to change without notice.

To: Hodder & Stoughton Ltd, Cash Sales Department, Bookpoint, 39 Milton Park, Abingdon, Oxon, OX14 4TD. If you have a credit card you may order by telephone – 01235 400414.

E-mail address: orders@bookpoint.co.uk

Please enclose a cheque or postal order made payable to Bookpoint Ltd to the value of the cover price and allow the following for postage and packaging:

UK & BFPO: £4.30 for one book; £6.30 for two books; £8.30 for three books.

OVERSEAS & EIRE: £4.80 for one book; £7.10 for 2 or 3 books (surface mail).

Name: ....

Address: ....

....

If you would prefer to pay by credit card, please complete:

Please debit my Visa/Mastercard/Diner's Card/American Express (delete as appropriate) card no:

❑❑❑❑❑❑❑❑❑❑❑❑❑❑❑❑

Signature .... Expiry Date ....